Scary Snakes

by Monica Hughes

Editoria[illegible] ick

CONTENTS

Words in **bold** are explained in the glossary.

Meet the snakes

Snakes have a dry, **scaly** skin.

As they grow, their skin gets too small and comes off.

They have new skin underneath.

Snakes don't have eyelids. They sleep with their eyes open.

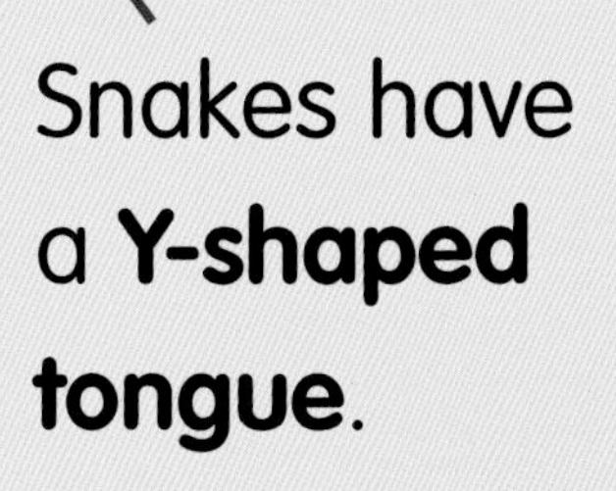

Snakes have a **Y-shaped tongue**.

Snake babies

Some snakes lay eggs.

The eggs are soft.

Snakes lay their eggs in a hole or in a nest made of leaves.

Baby snakes hatch from the eggs.

Some snakes do not lay eggs.

They give birth to baby snakes.

King cobra

The king cobra is **venomous**.

It is the biggest venomous snake in the world.

The king cobra hunts and eats birds, rats and other snakes.

It kills them with its venom.

It lays eggs in a nest.

Adder

The adder is a venomous snake too.

It eats small animals like
rats and lizards.

Sometimes it chases its **prey**.
Sometimes it hides and then attacks.

The adder gives birth to about
20 baby snakes at one time.

Royal python

This snake eats prey like rats and gerbils.

It wraps its body around the prey, then squeezes it to death.

The royal python lays eggs
in a hole or between rocks.

Rattlesnake

The rattlesnake lives in hot deserts.

It eats birds, rats and mice. It bites its prey with its venomous fangs.

It has hard scales on its tail that rattle.

The rattlesnake gives birth to baby snakes.

Y-shaped tongue

Anaconda

The anaconda is the heaviest snake in the world.

It eats pigs and deer.

It wraps its body around the prey. Then it squeezes the prey to death.

Anaconda

Y-shaped tongue

Anacondas give birth to baby snakes.

Emerald tree boa

The **emerald** tree boa lives in rainforests.

It eats birds and small animals.

The emerald tree boa gives birth to baby snakes.

The baby snakes are red, yellow or orange.

They turn green after one year.

Baby

Corn snake

The corn snake lives up trees and hides under rocks.

It is not venomous. It makes a good pet!

It eats rats and mice.

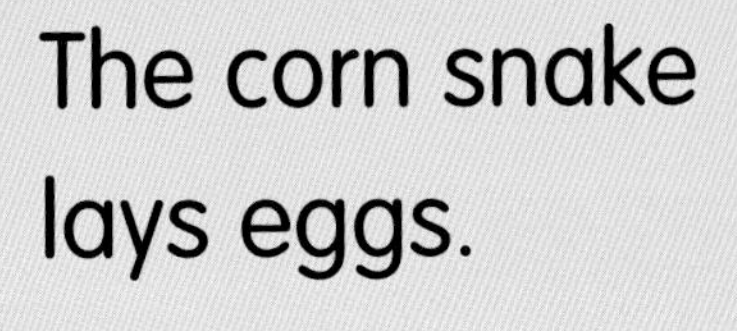

The corn snake
lays eggs.

Baby snakes
hatch after
60 days.

Glossary

emerald
A bright green colour.

prey
Something that is hunted and killed for food.

scaly

Covered with tough little plates or scales.

venomous

Has dangerous poison that can hurt or kill.

Y-shaped tongue

A tongue that is split at the end.

Index

First published in Great Britain in 2008 by **ticktock Media Ltd.**,
Unit 2, Orchard Business Centre, North Farm Road, Tunbridge Wells, Kent TN2 3XF
ISBN 978 1 84696 762 7 pbk
Printed in China

A CIP catalogue record for this book is available from the British Library.

We would like to thank: Penny Worms, Shirley Bickler, Suzanne Baker and the National Literacy Trust.

Picture credits (t=top, b=bottom, c=centre, l-left, r=right, OFC= outside front cover)
FLPA: 18-19. Shutterstock: 10-11, 14, 20t. Superstock: OFC, 7, 8, 15, 16-17.
ticktock photography: OFC, 4, 5, 6, 12, 13, 14-15c, 20b, 21.

Every effort has been made to trace the copyright holders, and we apologise in advance for any unintentional omissions. We would be pleased to insert the appropriate acknowledgements in any subsequent edition of this publication.